T0370432

Divine Comedy

Sacred Presence
in
Irreverent Humor

PHILIP KRILL

authorHOUSE®

AuthorHouse™
1663 Liberty Drive
Bloomington, IN 47403
www.authorhouse.com
Phone: 833-262-8899

Published by AuthorHouse 07/09/2024

ISBN: 979-8-8230-2923-0 (sc)
ISBN: 979-8-8230-2924-7 (e)

Print information available on the last page.

To

Barb Miller

A Sacred Presence in my life
who, in spite of herself, laughs at my irreverent humor

"Angels can fly because they take themselves lightly."

G. K. Chesterton, *Orthodoxy*

Contents

Introduction

If, as Chesterton says, 'angels can fly because they take themselves lightly,' then it behooves us to 'lighten up' if we wish to come close to God. No one ever entered God's Presence taking themselves more seriously than the One who beckons them forward. The kingdom of God is a Paradise of peace and joy. Funeral faces are not permitted.

The closest we can get to heaven on earth is to be filled with joy. And, for those who have sought in vain to find joy in religion, humor is the next best thing to connect with the Divine. Churches are emptying for want of heavenly joy, yet Starbucks and other such establishments are filled because they offer quick companionship and an atmosphere of light-heartedness. Grim-faced preachers could learn a lot from those friendly, inked-up baristas.

Question: Where do we find God? Answer: Wherever one person is fully present to another. Presence creates a mystical space in which angels delight and where the Spirit descends. Presence is a mystery of unrestricted openness filled with heavenly light. No one can abide in Presence and not be suffused with a joy that comes directly from God.

This book is an invitation to laugh your way into Presence. My prayer for you is that, dipping into this book, you will lighten up and fly with the angels into the joyful Presence of God.

20 June 2024

Woody Allen

Some drink deeply from the river of knowledge. Others only gargle.

Meditation

Thinking causes suffering, while simply being present brings peace. Presence is the living water quenching our spiritual thirst.

Prayer

Inundate us with the life-giving water of Presence, O God. Invite us to drink deeply of Your spiritual elixir.

In my next life, I want to live backwards. Start out dead and finish off as an orgasm.

Meditation

Learning to be present is an ecstatic experience. Presence is a participation in the ecstasy of God.

Prayer

Draw us into the ecstasy of Presence, O God. Save us from death by a million thoughts.

We stand at a crossroads. One path leads to despair, the other to destruction. Let's hope we make the right choice.

Meditation

There are no good options for those who cannot feel the difference between 'being present' and thinking.

Prayer

Move us beyond thinking into Presence, O God. Keep us from destruction and despair with the 'Power of the Now'.[1]

·

---

[1] Borrowed from the title of Eckhart Tolle's book, *Power of the Now*.

I didn't believe in reincarnation in my past life, and I still don't.

Meditation

Past lives are for those who have not transitioned from thinking to Presence. In the eternal Now, our true, unchanging identity is revealed.

Prayer

Help us live fully in the present moment, O God. In Presence, show the face we had before we were born.[2]

---

[2] Paraphrase of the famous Zen koan known as 'Original Face': 'Show me your original face, the face you had before your parents were born.'

There are worse things in life than death. Have you ever spent an evening with an insurance salesman?

Meditation

Apart from Presence, life is living death. Everyday worries kill those who have not yet discovered the difference between thinking and Presence.

Prayer

Raise us above the problems of the workaday world, O God. Deliver us from perpetual worry with the blessed grace of Presence.

I am not afraid of death. I just don't want to be there when it happens.

Meditation

Abiding in self-transcendence, we pass from death to life. In Presence, we discover a deathless identity.

Prayer

Perfect Presence drives out fear, O God. In Presence, deliver us from our fear of death.

My one regret in life is that I am not someone else.

Meditation

We imitate others until we discover our true identity in Presence. Presence is the antidote to codependence.

Prayer

Save us from odious comparisons with others, O God. Show us that to compare is to despair.

The meaning of life is that nobody knows the meaning of life.

Meditation

The search for meaning is inherently futile. 'What you seek, is seeking you.'[3]

Prayer

Teach us that 'You are closer to us than we are to ourselves,'[4] O God. Reveal Yourself in the experience of Presence.

---

[3] Famous quote of Sufi poet, Jalaluddin Rūmī
[4] St. Augustine, *Confessions* III, 6, 11.

If God exists, I hope he has a good excuse ... the worst that you can say about him is that basically he's an underachiever.

Meditation

All concepts of 'God' are flawed. 'God' is not an 'object' but the uncreated Source and Ground (*Ursprung*)[5] of all possible objects.

Prayer

Bless us with an enlightened a-theism, O God. Reveal Yourself in Presence as the ineffable Origin of existence.

---

[5] See Philip Krill, *Ursprung: Intuitions from God-Knows-Where.*

I don't believe in the afterlife, although I am bringing a change of underwear.

Meditation

Afterlife is a surrogate for the experience of *eternal* life. 'Heaven's not beyond the clouds, it's just beyond our fears,'[6] i.e, in Presence.

Prayer

In Presence, free us from our concerns about the afterlife, O God. Show us that 'the kingdom of God is within'.[7]

---

[6] A line from Garth Brooks' song, *Bellau Wood*.
[7] Luke 17:21.

Erma Bombeck

Seize the moment. Remember all those women on the 'Titanic' who waved off the dessert cart.

Meditation

To the hedonist, 'seize the moment' means 'get all you can while the getting is good'. To the mystic, 'seize the moment' means 'abide in Presence.'

Prayer

Sustain in us present moment awareness, O God. Show us that every moment is pregnant with eternal life.

Never go to a doctor whose office plants have died.

Meditation

How we do anything is how we do everything. Abiding in Presence, all our actions radiate love.

Prayer

Grant us integrity of action, O God. In Presence, make our external efforts reflect our purity of heart.

The odds of going to the store for a loaf of bread and coming out with only a loaf of bread are three billion to one.

Meditation

Greed spoils everything. Only in Presence are we free of grasping and covetousness.

Prayer

Show us the beauty of 'desire-less action,'[8] O God. In Presence, inspire us to give without regard to the fruits of our giving.

---

[8] *Nishkama Karma* is self-less or desire-less action, i.e., action performed without any expectation of fruits or results.

No one ever died from sleeping in an unmade bed.

Meditation

We are often blind to the pettiness of our concerns. Presence dispels our blindness.

Prayer

Draw us ever more deeply into Presence, O God. Show us that Presence is 'the one thing necessary,'[9] for getting our priorities right.

---

[9] Luke 10:42.

Did you ever notice that the first piece of luggage on the carousel never belongs to anyone?

Meditation

Fear of being 'left out' or 'left behind' is the curse of humankind. Presence disarms us of such fears.

Prayer

Fill us with the patience and peace that flows from Presence, O God. Show us that Presence is a share in the Love that 'casts out all fear'.[10]

---

[10] 1 John 4:18.

I come from a family where gravy is considered a beverage.

Meditation

Comfort eating is eventually counter-productive. Presence - 'the bread come down from heaven'[11] - is the comfort food that truly satisfies.

Prayer

Teach us to feast on Presence, O God. 'Give us this bread always'.[12]

---

[11] John 6:50.
[12] John 6:34.

Guilt: the gift that keeps on giving.

Meditation

Guilt is the underbelly of gratitude. Presence banishes guilt and fills us with gratitude and joy.

Prayer

Turn our 'tears into rejoicing,'[13] O God. In Presence, transform our guilt into graciousness and peace.

---

[13] Psalm 126:5.

He who laughs ... lasts.

Meditation

Laughter is God's elixir. In Presence, it's impossible not to smile.

Prayer

Flood us with the joy of Presence, O God. Show us that the ironies of life are flashes of a bliss-filled eternity.

There's nothing sadder in this world than to awake Christmas morning and not be a child.

Meditation

We must 'become like little children' to enter the kingdom of God.[14] Presence is the playground for the friends of God.

Prayer

Sustain us with child-like joy, O God. In Presence, make every day Christmas.

---

[14] Matthew 18:3.

I've exercised with women so thin that buzzards followed them to their cars.

Meditation

Compulsive behavior is disguised as despondency. Presence imparts the peace that saves us from desperation.

Prayer

Deliver us from the illusion of self-improvement, O God. Reveal Presence as the real power of positive change.

Rodney Dangerfield

When I was born I was so ugly the doctor slapped my mother.

Meditation

Not all self-love is egoistic. We can only 'love others as ourselves' if we do just that: love ourselves as God loves us.

Prayer

Show us the meaning of true self-esteem, O God. Helps us to view ourselves and others through the lens of Divine Mercy.

When I was born ... the doctor came out to the waiting room and said to my father ... I'm very sorry. We did everything we could ... but he pulled through.

Meditation

Many are they who rue the day they were born.[15] Such regrets evaporate once we discover the power of Presence.

Prayer

Awaken us to our true identity in Presence, O God. Reveal our eternal identity as Your beloved children.

---

[15] See Job 10:18; Jeremiah 20:14; cf. Mark 14:21.

When I was a kid my parents moved a lot, but I always found them.

Meditation

It's impossible to disown our heritage, but neither are we defined by it. In Presence, we discover our true, transcendent identity in God.

Prayer

Show us who we are beyond the markers of family and fortune, O God. Help us to know ourselves as You know us.

I told my psychiatrist that everyone hates me. He said I was being ridiculous - everyone hasn't met me yet.

Meditation

We see others, not as it is, but as we are. Only a deified vision,[16] acquired in Presence, saves us from seeing others in a negative light.

Prayer

Purify our mendacity with Your Mercy, O God. Grant us a heavenly vision so we can disavow all hate.

---

[16] See Philip Krill, *Deified Vision: Towards an Anagogical Catholicism.*

When I was a kid, I had no friends. I remember the see-saw. I had to keep running from one end to the other.

Meditation

Loneliness is spiritually lethal. Presence is the prescription for broken hearts.

Prayer

Save us from isolation, O God. Banish our loneliness with the light and joy of Presence.

My wife and I were happy for 20 years. Then we met.

Meditation

Regret and remorse rule the past until we discover the power of Presence. In Presence, 'we neither regret the past nor wish to close the door on it.'[17]

Prayer

Show us that the past is a cancelled check, and the future a promissory note, O God. Teach us to live nowhere but in the present moment.

---

[17] One of the 'Promises' of *Alcoholics Anonymous*.

I haven't spoken to my wife in years. I didn't want to interrupt her.

Meditation

To listen, we must be fully present. This is a gift and a skill that escapes most people.

Prayer

Grant us a listening ear, O God. Reveal Presence as the key to communion.

My wife has to be the worst cook. In my house, we pray after we eat.

Meditation

Gratitude, to enrich us, cannot be an afterthought. In Presence, we experience gratitude as a way of life, not a polite addendum.

Prayer

Grant us grateful hearts, O God. In Presence, make our lives a perpetual Thanksgiving.

I asked my old man if I could go ice-skating on the lake. He told me, 'Wait til it gets warmer.'

Meditation

Mendacity is our default position until Presence makes its power known. Presence transforms malice into divine mercy.

Prayer

Purify our hearts with the power of Presence, O God. Show us that in Presence, fear, doubt, and insecurity disappear.

Once, when I was lost, I asked a policeman to help me find my parents. I said to him, 'Do you think we'll ever find them?' He answered, 'I don't know, kid. There are so many places they can hide.'

Meditation

There is nowhere we can run where we can hide from ourselves. In Presence, we learn to stop running.

Prayer

Bring us into the Peace of Presence, O God. Show us that in Presence we discover what we've been looking for all our lives.

Groucho Marx

I refuse to join any club that would have me as a member.

Meditation

Failing self-appreciation, self-deprecation is all we have left. In Presence, we love ourselves and everyone else.

Prayer

Take us beyond inner criticism, O God. Bathe our spirits in the benevolent Light of Presence.

The secret of life is honesty and fair dealing. If you can fake that, you've got it made.

Meditation

Who can be completely honest without shame? Only those self-possessed in Presence.

Prayer

Grant us the disarming honesty found in Presence, O God. Show us how to be candid without caveats or condescension.

If you are not having fun, you are doing something wrong.

Meditation

Nothing done without joy is ultimately worth doing. Make your vocation your vacation, and you'll never work a day in your life.

Prayer

You reveal Presence as the 'narrow way' leading to Your kingdom of joy, O God.[18] Grant us the joy of doing all things with Presence.

---

[18] See Matthew 7:14; John 15:11.

When you're in jail, a good friend will be trying to bail you out. A best friend will be in the cell next to you saying, 'Damn, that was fun.'

Meditation

Presence creates communion, even among thieves. Remorse and regret are unknown to those abiding in Presence.

Prayer

Teach us to assess good and evil from the standpoint of Presence, O God. In Presence, teach us to treat 'those two imposters just the same.'[19]

---

[19] A phrase borrowed from Rudyard Kipling's poem, *If.*

Marriage is a wonderful institution, but who wants to live in an institution?

Meditation

Roles imprison us, but Presence sets us free. In Presence, we see the falsehood and futility of a role-driven, institution-defined life.

Prayer

Awaken us to our identity beyond the roles we assume, O God. In Presence, free us from socially-constructed images of ourselves.

Blessed are the cracked, for they shall let in the light.

Meditation

Presence is the Light that reveals and fills the cracks in our facade. With the collapse of the *persona*, our true personhood can emerge.

Prayer

In Presence, remove our masks of ego, O God. Destroy the false fronts keeping us from looking, angel-like, upon Your face and those of others.[20]

---

[20] See Matthew 18:10.

She got her looks from her father. He's a plastic surgeon.

Meditation

Physical beauty is as fleeting as it is arresting. In Presence, we behold beauty that never fades.

Prayer

Beautify our hearts with the Light of Presence, O God. Help us see the world bathed in Your eternal loveliness.

There's one way to find out if a man is honest - ask him. If he says, 'Yes,' you know he is a crook.

Meditation

Self-deception is our default position apart from Presence. In Presence, we see without pretense and accept without judgment.

Prayer

Deliver us into the blessed space of Presence, O God. Teach us to rest in Presence where love and truth are one.

Time wounds all heels.

Meditation

Time is God's way of softening hearts and smoothing out rough edges. The perfection of time is Presence.

Prayer

Show us that every moment of time is a point of access into Presence, O God. Establish us in the blissful state of present awareness.

A clown is like aspirin, only he works twice as fast.

Meditation

Tomfoolery often accomplishes what intensity cannot. In Presence, we recognize the foolishness of our best-laid plans.

Prayer

Teach us to lighten up, O God. Show us that in Presence we accomplish much without taking ourselves too seriously.

Phyllis Diller

I spent seven hours in a beauty shop ... and that was for the estimate.

Meditation

Self-estimation is inevitably flawed. Our real worth is disclosed only in Presence.

Prayer

Reveal us to ourselves, O God. In Presence, show us 'the name no one knows except the one who receives it.'[21]

---

[21] See Revelation 2:17

You know you're old when someone compliments you on your alligator shoes, and you're barefoot.

Meditation

Presence reveals aging to be a thing of beauty. In Presence, we experience a letting-go that is truly divine.

Prayer

Teach us to embrace the aging process, O God. Show us that, in Presence, You 'make all things new.'[22]

---

[22] See Revelation 21:5.

Housework can't kill you, but why take a chance?

Meditation

Maturity means learning to separate the 'trivial many' from the 'vital few.' Our discernment is clear when we abide in Presence.

Prayer

Teach us not to sweat the little things, O God. In Presence, show us the 'one thing necessary.'[23]

---

[23] See Luke 10:42.

Most children threaten at times to run away from home. This is the only thing that keeps some parents going.

Meditation

Apart from Presence, we struggle in relationships. In Presence, we relax into contented communion with ourselves and others.

Prayer

Grant us the peace that comes from Presence, O God. Transform our relationships with others into a holy communion.

I don't know how you feel about old age ... but in my case, I didn't even see it coming. It hit me from the rear.

Meditation

In Presence, we swim in an ocean of life-giving beneficence. Outside of Presence, we resemble dead, bloated fish on the beach.

Prayer

Fill us with the joy and freedom of swimming in Presence, O God. Draw us deeply into this ocean of divine love.

Health - what my friends are always drinking to before they fall down.

Meditation

Self-sabotage is a common commodity. In Presence, self-care replaces self-sabotage.

Prayer

Show us that our addictions are aspirations for euphoria, O God. Show us that such aspirations are fulfilled only in Presence.

[On plastic surgery:] When I die, God won't know me. There are no two parts of my body the same age.

Meditation

Facial reconstruction belies the need for a spiritual makeover. In Presence, both our bodies and souls are naturally beautified.

Prayer

Beautify us from the inside out, O God. In Presence, make our faces shine with Your divine glory.[24]

---

[24] See Exodus 34:35.

Never go to bed mad. Stay up and fight.

Meditation

The game of tit-for-tat never ends until we discover Presence. In Presence, the '4R's' (resentment, rage, retribution and retaliation) cease to exist.

Prayer

Deliver us from impulsive reactivity, O God. In Presence, unmask the 'myth of redemptive violence.'[25]

---

[25] A phrase coined by Walter Wink (1999), *'The Myth of Redemptive Violence'*. On-line: https://www.goshen.edu/~joannab/women/wink99.pdf.

When you play spin the bottle, if they don't want to kiss you, they have to give you a quarter. Well, hell, by the time I was twelve years old I owned my own home.

Meditation

We can't purchase love. The Love we experience in Presence is 'the pearl of great price' which no amount of money can buy.[26]

Prayer

Bequeath us the priceless pearl of Presence, O God. Let Presence be our sole inheritance.

---

[26] See Matthew 13:46.

You know what keeps me humble? Mirrors!

Meditation

Our self-images are always distorted. In Presence, we experience ourselves perfectly reflected in God's Divine Mirror.[27]

Prayer

Reveal our pre-eternal perfection in You, O God. In Presence, show us our inherent beauty in the mirror of Your infinite Love.

---

[27] See: *"Divine Mirror Meditation as Read by Richard Rohr."* YouTube, 26 Jan. 2020, www.youtube.com/watch?v=KbcXms6WR0k. Accessed 7 June 2024.

George Carlin

Just cause you got the monkey off your back doesn't mean the circus has left town.

Meditation

Character defects do not disappear all at once. In Presence, we discover God's timing is always perfect.

Prayer

Make us comfortable with continual conversion, O God. In Presence, give us patience with personal transformation.

The real reason that we can't have the Ten Commandments in a courthouse: You cannot post 'Thou shalt not steal, 'Thou shalt not commit adultery,' and 'Thou shalt not lie' in a building full of lawyers, judges, and politicians. It creates a hostile work environment.

Meditation

Apart from Presence, the truth hurts. In Presence, the truth about ourselves is as self-evident as it is forgiving.

Prayer

Those who live in glass houses should not throw stones. Presence disarms us of the need to cast aspersions.

Some people have no idea what they're doing, and a lot of them are really good at it.

Meditation

Stupidity takes itself too seriously. Presence reveals that much of what we do is 'chronicles of wasted time.'[28]

Prayer

Deliver us from our tunnel vision, O God. In Presence, usher us into Your House of Divine Wisdom.[29]

---

[28] Phrase borrowed from the title of Malcom Muggeridge's book, *Chronicles of Wasted Time: An Autobiography*.
[29] See Proverbs 14:1.

Religion has convinced people that there's an invisible man living in the sky ... Who watches everything you do every minute of every day. And the invisible man has a list of ten specific things he doesn't want you to do. And if you do any of these things, he will send you to a special place, of burning and fire and smoke and torture and anguish for you to live forever, and suffer, and suffer, and burn, and scream, until the end of time. But he loves you. He loves you. He loves you and he needs money.

Meditation

For many, religion is a matter of purchasing spiritual life-insurance against God. In Presence, God frees us from all such fears.[30]

Prayer

Remind us that 'love has no religion,' O God.[31] In Presence, reveal Your Love that 'passes all understanding'.[32]

---

[30] See 1 John 4:18.

[31] Quote borrowed from Mawlānā Jalāl al-Dīn al-Rūmī. See Philip Krill, *Mawlānā: Contemplating Love with Rumi.*

[32] Philippians. 4:7

Have you ever noticed that anybody driving slower than you is an idiot, and anyone going faster than you is a maniac?

Meditation

Apart from Presence, criticism comes naturally to us. Presence reveals criticism as a betrayal of our true nature as 'gods in God.'[33]

Prayer

Blind us to the character defects of others, O God. Establish us in Presence where harsh judgments are impossible.

---

[33] A common theme in the writings of the early church fathers. The idea of deification ('gods in God') was the central point of the nascent life of the Christian East, the point around which revolved all the questions of dogmatics, ethics, and mysticism.

The word bi-partisan usually means some larger-than-usual deception is being carried out.

Meditation

The whole world is hypnotized by the 'myth of redemptive violence.'[34] Presence awakens us from the nightmare of corporate delusion.

Prayer

Extricate us from the unending cycle of retaliation, O God. In Presence, show us the way out of mutual destruction.

---

[34] See above, n. 18.

The caterpillar does all the work, but the butterfly gets all the publicity.

Meditation

Presence is our spiritual cocoon. Gestating there, we emerge miraculously transformed.

Prayer

Enclose us in the divine incubator of Presence, O God. In Presence, make us Your 'new creations'.[35]

---

[35] See 2 Corinthians 5:17.

There are three kinds of people: those who can count, and those who cannot.

Meditation

Our actions often belie our words. Presence purifies us of all duplicity.

Prayer

Purify our hearts with Presence, O God. In Presence, make us persons of perfect integrity.

Here's all you have to know about men and women: women are crazy, men are stupid. And the main reason women are crazy is that men are stupid.

Meditation

The battle of the sexes has no resolution apart from Presence. Presence brings peace where before there was only mutual provocation.

Prayer

Show us that Presence is 'the answer to all our problems today', O God. In Presence, teach us how to 'live and let live'.[36]

---

[36] Two mottos borrowed from *Alcoholics Anonymous*.

Ever wonder about those people who spend $2 apiece on those little bottles of Evian water? Try spelling Evian backward.

Meditation

Human naïveté knows no bounds. Presence awakens us to our inveterate gullibility.

Prayer

Make us less susceptible to ignorant decisions, O God. In Presence, grant us a 'second naïveté'[37] - one filled with learned wisdom.

---

[37] 'Beyond rational and critical thinking, we need to be called again. This can lead to the discovery of a "second naïveté," which is a return to the joy of our first naïveté, but now totally new, inclusive, and mature thinking.' (Paul Ricœur), cited by Richard Rohr, *'The Ability to Hold Paradox.'* Center for Action and Contemplation, 24 Aug. 2020, cac.org/daily-meditations/the-ability-to-hold-paradox-2020-08-24/. Accessed 7 June 2024.

Jay Leno

The crime problem in New York is getting really serious. The other day the Statue of Liberty had both hands up.

Meditation

Crime is the common condition in a world oblivious to Presence. Presence replaces crime with holy communion.

Prayer

Transform us with the power of Your Presence, O God. In Presence, free us from our crimes.

We should make politicians dress like race car drivers - when they get money, make them wear the company logos on their suits.

Meditation

Politics is the arena of bribery and blackmail. Presence is the arena of selfless love and altruistic service.

Prayer

Lift us above the political polemics, O God. In Presence, show us 'a new city, coming down out of heaven, prepared as a bride adorned for her husband'.[38]

---

[38] Revelation 21:2.

Yesterday morning Facebook was temporarily offline, leaving millions of workers unable to do anything except their jobs.

Meditation

Distractions sometimes occupy the lion's share of our time. Presence focuses us completely on that which matters most.

Prayer

Fill our days with meaningful moments, O God. In Presence, show us that every moment is filled with meaning.

The Supreme Court has ruled that they cannot have a nativity scene in Washington, D.C. This wasn't for any religious reasons. They couldn't find three wise men and a virgin.

Meditation

Secular society leaves little room for the sacred. In Presence, the secular world is itself sacred.

Prayer

Illumine our pedestrian world with Presence, O God. Let the divine Light of Presence make visible the sacred depths of ordinary life.

At the Sharper Image store, I saw a body fat analyzer. Didn't that used to be called a mirror?

Meditation

Many are loathe to look at themselves in the mirror. Presence is the spiritual mirror where shame cannot obscure the beauty of our souls.

Prayer

'Before the foundation of the world', You have 'chosen us to be holy and blameless in Your sight',[39] O God. In Presence, reveal our eternal beauty.

---

[39] Ephesians 1:4.

A Canadian psychologist is selling a video that teaches you how to test your dog's IQ. Here's how it works: if you spend $12.99 for the video, your dog is smarter than you.

Meditation

Animals know instinctively; human intelligence is much more deliberative and more easily deceived.

Prayer

Grant us the intuitive knowing that comes from Presence, O God. In Presence, give us a share of Your divine Wisdom (*Sophia*).

President James Garfield could write in Latin with one hand while writing in Greek with the other. I would give my right arm to be ambidextrous.

Meditation

Polyglots amaze us with their facility with languages. In Presence, we discover a more amazing language of silence.

Prayer

Teach us the language of the Spirit, O God. In Presence, teach us to speak with the 'tongues of angels'.[40]

---

[40] 1 Corinthians 13:1.

The Washington Bullets are changing their name. They don't want their team to be associated with crime. From now on, they'll just be known as the Bullets.

Meditation

Politics is the art of blaming others. In Presence, there is no one to blame, not even ourselves.

Prayer

Grant us a share in Your blameless Life, O God. In Presence, make us 'partakers of Your divine nature',[41] which is love.

---

[41] 2 Peter 1:4.

You know who must be very secure in their masculinity? Male ladybugs.

Meditation

As sexual identity becomes blurred in secular society, our eternal identity remains unchanged. In Presence, we discover who we are before time began.

Prayer

Awaken us to our pre-eternal identity in You, O God. In Presence, show us who we are 'before the foundation of the world'.[42]

---

[42] John 17:24.

A German psychologist says that women talk more than men because they have a bigger vocabulary. But, it evens out because men only listen half the time.

Meditation

'Men are from Mars, and women are from Venus'.[43] Presence delivers men and women from the battle of the sexes.

Prayer

School us in compassionate communication, O God. In Presence, show us the power of active listening.

---

[43] Phrase borrowed from the title of John Gray's book by the same name.

Jerry Seinfeld

Men want the same thing from their underwear that they want from women: a little bit of support, and a little bit of freedom.

Meditation

Love is an alchemy of the 'desire for union' and the 'need for freedom'. Only in Presence does this alchemy produce relationship gold.

Prayer

Show us that freedom is the key to intimacy, O God. In Presence, show us that 'letting go' is the way of divine love.

Surveys show that the #1 fear of Americans is public speaking. #2 is death. That means that at a funeral, the average American would rather be in the casket than doing the eulogy.

Meditation

The fear of death renders most of us speechless. Presence delivers us from our 'slavery to the fear of death'.[44]

Prayer

Banish our fear of death, O God. In Presence, cause us to say, 'O death, where is your victory? O death, where is your sting?'.[45]

---

[44] Hebrews 2:15.
[45] 1 Corinthians 15:55.

Where lipstick is concerned, the important thing is not color, but to accept God's final word on where your lips end.

Meditation

Cosmetic surgery bespeaks a soul sickness. Only Presence can bring a completely natural smile to our faces.

Prayer

Transfigure our faces with Your uncreated Light, O God.[46] In Presence, change us 'into Your likeness, from one degree of glory to another'.[47]

---

[46] See Exodus 34:35; Mark 9:3.
[47] 2 Corinthians 3:18.

There is no such thing as fun for the whole family.

Meditation

'The family that prays together, stays together'.[48] Otherwise, family fights are no fun.

Prayer

Save us from internecine in-fighting, O God. In Presence, turn our family feuds into occasions for holy communion.

---

[48] Saying attributed to Fr. Patrick Peyton in his world-wide family rosary campaign.

If a book about failures doesn't sell, is it a success?

Meditation

Acknowledging failure is always a success. In the world of the Spirit, surrender is victory, and acceptance is its own reward.

Prayer

Show us that admitting failure is always a spiritual triumph, O God. In Presence, reveal acceptance as the true path to peace.

Being a good husband is like being a good stand-up comic - you need ten years before you can even call yourself a beginner.

Meditation

In Presence, we are always beginners. 'When we've been there ten thousand years it's as if we've just begun.'[49]

Prayer

Deepen our experience of Presence O God, for in Presence You impart to us a wisdom that a lifetime of worldly learning cannot give.

---

[49] Paraphrase of the final verse of *Amazing Grace*.

If you can't be kind, at least have the decency to be vague.

Meditation

Violence, vilification, and prevarication are the ways of the world. In Presence, everything but kindness disappears.

Prayer

Teach us to be neither unkind nor untoward, O God. In Presence, make us instruments of Your 'everlasting kindness'.[50]

---

[50] See Psalm 136; Titus 3:4.

I think vacations are mostly completely stupid. Going to have coffee with a friend, you're probably going to have more fun than if you go to Aruba.

Meditation

If we make our vocation our vacation, we'll never work a day in our lives. Presence is the vocation ('calling') that makes every day a vacation.

Prayer

Inspire us to hearken to Your summons to Presence, O God. Show us that in Presence we find the fulfillment that vacations falsely promise.

People who read the tabloids deserve to be lied to.

Meditation

Karma means everyone eventually gets what they deserve. Presence delivers us from the logic of 'what goes around, comes around.'

Prayer

Save us from our 'dog eat dog' world, O God. In Presence, transform our fatalism into 'the fulfillment of all desire'.[51]

---

[51] See Psalm 20:4.

What is this obsession people have with books? They put them in their houses like they're trophies. What do you need it for after you read it?

Meditation

Books on a shelf are no replacement for wisdom in the heart. Presence is the library of the spirit.

Prayer

Infuse us with divine intuition, O God. In Presence, reveal the Love that 'no eye can see, no ear can hear, and no human mind can understand'.[52]

---

[52] See 1 Corinthians 2:9.

Roseanne Barr

Half the world's starving; the other half is trying to lose weight.

Meditation

We live in a schizophrenic world. Presence saves us from a teeter-totter existence.

Prayer

Save us from ambivalence, confusion and indecision, O God. In Presence, give us the 'peace that passes all understanding'.[53]

---

[53] Philippians 4:7.

I'm not upset about my divorce. I'm only upset that I'm not a widow.

Meditation

Resentment is like drinking poison and hoping our adversary will die. Presence makes holding grudges impossible.

Prayer

Free us from our anger and envy, O God. In Presence, purify our hearts with Your Light and Love.

As a housewife, I feel that if the kids are still alive when my husband gets home from work, then hey, I've done my job.

Meditation

Resentments are driven by our role-driven identities. Defining oneself as 'I am this' or 'I am that' is to obscure one's true identity as 'I am'.

Prayer

Show us that we are 'they who are' *in* You who is 'I AM'.[54] In Presence, reveal our deepest identity in You.[55]

---

[54] See Exodus 3:14.
[55] See Colossians 3:3.

Women complain about PMS, but I think of it as the only time of the month when I can be myself.

Meditation

Pain sometimes gives us permission to be ourselves. In Presence, we are never anything but our real selves.

Prayer

Show us that emotional outbursts belie a deeper desire for peace, O God. In Presence, give us the 'peace the world cannot give'.[56]

---

[56] John 14:27.

My husband says, 'Roseanne, don't you think we ought to talk about our sexual problems?' Like I'm gonna turn off Wheel of Fortune for that.

Meditation

Everything is sacred or nothing is sacred. Apart from Presence, life is a series of trivial entertainments.

Prayer

Imbue us with the sacredness of the present moment, O God. In Presence, help us 'see the world in a grain of sand and a heaven in a wild flower'.[57]

---

[57] The first line of William Blake's poem, *Auguries of Innocence*.

There isn't a problem on this earth that a doughnut cannot make better.

Meditation

Sensual satisfaction is the world's way of feeding our spiritual hunger. Presence is the 'true bread come down from heaven'.[58]

Prayer

Show us that most of our problems 'are of our own making',[59] O God. In Presence, satisfy our hunger with 'the food which endures to eternal life'.[60]

---

[58] See John 6:32-58.
[59] A phrase borrowed from the big book of *Alcoholics Anonymous*.
[60] John 6:27.

Being nuts is its own reward.

Meditation

It's good to be disillusioned in a world driven by illusions. 'No prophet is welcome'[61] when questioning the wisdom of the *status quo.*

Prayer

Show us we are not 'out of our minds'[62] when we oppose the world's ways, O God. Reveal Presence as our alternative to the world's insanity.

---

[61] Luke 4:24.
[62] Mark 3:21.

I consider myself to be a pretty good judge of people ... that's why I don't like any of them.

Meditation

No one is completely likable when we see them on the surface. Presence reveals a depth to every person that compels our respect.

Prayer

Teach us to think of others 'not as human beings do, but as You do',[63] O God. In Presence, show us the inherent goodness of every person.

---

[63] Matthew 16:23.

I'm fat and proud of it. If someone asks me how my diet is going, I say 'Fine - how was your lobotomy?'

Meditation

So much of life is tit-for-tat, action and reaction. Presence deliver us from escalating insults and imitative intimidation.

Prayer

Show us our mothers were not wrong to wash our mouths out with soap at times, O God. In Presence, make us kind in word and deed.

My husband and I didn't sign a pre-nuptial agreement. We signed a mutual suicide pact.

Meditation

Relationships can be emotional suicide pacts for those unfamiliar with Presence. In Presence, everyone is 'my mother, brother and sister'.[64]

Prayer

Redeem our relationships with Presence, O God. In Presence, disclose our inseparable connection with every person we meet.

---

[64] Mark 3:35.

Yogi Berra

If you don't know where you are going, you might wind up someplace else.

Meditation

Ready, fire, aim - this is the *modus operandi* of those unfamiliar with Presence. In Presence, we always know 'the next right thing'.

Prayer

Reveal Presence as the divine galaxy where our spiritual North Star can be found, O God. In Presence, direct us to Your 'kingdom within'.[65]

---

[65] Luke 17:21.

Trust your instincts. When you come to a fork in the road, take it.

Meditation

Arbitrary actions are the daily fare of those ignorant of Presence. In Presence, discernment replaces impulsive decision-making.

Prayer

Give us true discernment, O God. In Presence, gift us with a deified vision.[66]

---

[66] See above, n. 16.

Ninety percent of all mental errors are in your head.

Meditation

Untethered to Presence, the mind is a dangerous neighborhood. Don't go in there without adult supervision.

Prayer

Save us from mental masturbation, O God. Grant us the purity of vision that is found only in Presence.

Listen up, because I've got nothing to say and I'm only gonna to say it once.

Meditation

Just as some foods can be but empty calories, so can many words be vacuous bluster. In Presence, we mean what we say, and say what we mean.

Prayer

Grant us sincerity of speech, O God. In Presence, conform our words to the 'truth that sets us free'.[67]

---

[67] John 8:32.

When the waitress asked if I wanted my pizza cut into four or eight slices, I said, 'Four. I don't think I can eat eight.'

Meditation

'A rose is a rose is a rose'.[68] Reality is what it is, regardless of how we slice it up.

Prayer

Open our eyes to the actuality of things beneath our thoughts, O God. In Presence, show us that 'there lives the dearest freshness deep down things'.[69]

---

[68] A line from the writings of Gertrude Stein, first appearing in her poem, *Sacred Emily*.
[69] Gerard Manley Hopkins, *The Grandeur of God*.

Yogi Berra

You can observe a lot by just watching.

Meditation

Outside of Presence, we 'have eyes that do not see, ears that do not hear'.[70] In Presence, God gives us audio and visual clarity.

Prayer

Open our eyes to the invisible beauty of Presence, O God. In Presence, open our ears to the silent music[71] of the angels and saints.

---

[70] Psalm 115:5; Ezekiel 12:2.
[71] See William Johnston, S.J., *Silent Music: The Science of Meditation.*

If you don't set goals, you can't regret not reaching them.

Meditation

Actions performed without expectation of results bear the most fruit. In Presence, we learn to practice 'desire-less' effort.[72]

Prayer

Teach us the delight of detachment, O God. In Presence, show us that relinquishing results enriches our every effort.

---

[72] See above, n. 8.

You should always go to other people's funerals, otherwise, they won't come to yours.

Meditation

Funerals are the fabrications we use to deny the reality of death.[73] Presence reveals death as nothing to be feared.[74]

Prayer

Grant us a share in divine relinquishment,[75] O God. In Presence, show us that 'letting go' always results in being 'lifted up'.[76]

---

[73] See Ernest Becker, *The Denial of Death*.

[74] See Hebrews 2:15; Luke 12:4.

[75] *'Gelassenheit'* is a term, associated with Meister Eckhart, to describe 'divine releasement'. See Philip Krill, *Gelassenheit: Day-by-Day with Meister Eckhart*.

[76] See John 12:32.

In theory, there is no difference between theory and practice. In practice there is.

Meditation

Much of the world's wisdom is oxymoronic. Presence transforms morons into mystics.

Prayer

Dissolve the difference between theory and practice in Presence, O God. In Presence, make 'what we know' and 'what we do' seamlessly sacred.

The future ain't what it used to be.

Meditation

Future tripping is a place of refuge for those escaping the present moment. Presence is the only place where past and future cannot dominate us.

Prayer

Remove us from the endless cycle of past and future, O God. Show us that, in Presence, we experience an Eternal Now.[77]

---

[77] See Richard Rohr, 'The Eternal Now,' Center for Action and Contemplation. April 30, 2019. https://cac.org/daily-meditations/the-eternal-now-2019-04-30/.